I0052508

Welcome

Hey, glad to see you here! Thanks for picking up (in the figurative sense, of course) the Welcome To Your Independence freelance handbook. Thinking about going freelance? Not sure exactly how to go about it? Well, you are in luck! Having compiled AND CO's learnings from working with thousands of freelancers, Welcome To Your Independence was written precisely for individuals who are seeking to enter the world of freelancing as well as those who are looking to refine processes already in place. Whichever your starting point, Welcome To Your Independence aims to clearly and concisely guide you through the process of going freelance and making it as an independent worker.

CONTENT

INTRODUCTION

What is freelance?

Welcome To Your Independence explores the steps it takes to become a freelancer; but, what does it really mean to freelance? In the age of the gig economy, it seems as if everyone from your cousin to your best friend to even your dad is picking up side jobs here and there to make an extra buck. From the Uber driver to the part-time photographer, there is a plethora of individuals taking on new opportunities apart from their full time work. That being said, there isn't just one definition of freelancing.

At AND CO *we divide freelancers into three groups based on their workflow:*

PROJECT BASED WORKFLOW

This type of freelancer takes on projects with set start and end dates for B2B clients and includes designers, developers, writers etc.

SCHEDULING BASED WORKFLOW

These freelancers work on a calendar management basis, such as personal trainers and real estate agents, and more often these are B2C client relationships.

SHIFT BASED WORKFLOW

When the work involves set shifts and set customers, workers in this category have typically not chosen to be freelance, such as an Uber driver or TaskRabbit mover.

Throughout this book, we will focus on the project based workflow. We will address specifically the project based freelancer who is ready to take their skills and leap from working for someone else to working for themselves, to earning their own keep, and to welcoming their independence.

Whether you want to have control over your working hours in order to spend more time with your children, or if you are looking to work from anywhere and pick your own clients for a change, then listen up, because we are talking to you.

Why freelance?

Freelancing is one of the most rewarding choices you can make. It allows freedom, control, and incredible independence. It's also risky, hard work, and extremely challenging. But nothing will beat what it means to be your own boss.

People are choosing to go freelance every-day. Over 50 million Americans have chosen to embrace their independence. And we are excited to see you are considering the path as well. This book will guide you through the steps needed to take to make your freelance dreams a reality.

Take out a piece of paper. It doesn't have to be very large. Grab a pen. And write down exactly the reasons why you want to go freelance. Do it. Right now. That's the first step. Use clear language and make it legible! Here are some inspirational reasons for going freelance:

- Be your own boss

- Choose your own working hours

- Be free to work as you like

- Work from anywhere in the world

- Pick your own clients

- Up your earning potential

- Control your own destiny

- Build your confidence and your character

- Do the work that you love

And the list goes on, but ultimately did you write down your reason? Good! Because that is the most important nugget of truth that will carry you through when times get tough. It is also the reason that you should feel empowered right now to get the ball rolling and not delay your future! We're super excited to help lay the groundwork of what it takes to go from making the decision to welcoming your independence.

READY TO ROLL UP YOUR SLEEVES AND TAKE MATTERS INTO YOUR OWN HANDS?

GETTING THE PAPERWORK TOGETHER

Establish your business entity

Establishing the business entity for your business is a strong first step on the path to independence. You'll create an element of legal protection for your business and may enjoy some tax advantages as well. Let's explore the different options that are out there so that you can make an educated decision about which would be best for you.

SOLE PROPRIETORSHIP

A sole proprietorship is one of the most simple and common forms of business. While a sole proprietorship will help to make your tax filing a little more painless, it offers no protection against personal liability. With this type of entity, there is no clear distinction between the business and the owner. Only you are solely responsible for all debts, losses, liabilities, etc. Further, no formal action is needed in order to form a sole proprietorship.

As long as you are the only owner, this status is automatically attributed to you as a result of your business activities. A common case when it is good to choose to be a sole proprietor is if you wish to save money, do not expect the business to grow much, and have steady debt liabilities.

CO TIP:

When the sole proprietor has a spouse, the IRS treats the income as belonging to you and your spouse, but recognizes that only you own and run the business. Be careful that when you fill out any business registrations forms and especially when you fill out your Schedule C that you list only yourself and not your spouse. The IRS will be able to clearly identity the business as solely run by you, even though the income is joint.

S CORP

If you really want to protect your personal assets from creditors, an S Corp is a solid option in that regard. Furthermore, an S Corp means you avoid having to pay both personal and corporate taxes. An S Corp is responsible for paying an employee industry normal salary and also deducts payroll expenses such as federal taxes and FICA.

As a result of S Corp election, there are strict requirements one must uphold, including being a U.S. resident, having only one class of stock, having no more than 100 shareholders, and distributing profits and losses to shareholders in proportion to shareholders' interest.

Keep in mind, forming an S Corp is a costly endeavor and it only makes sense to become an S Corp if you anticipate making more than $150,000/year.

When tax season arrives, it is strongly advised that you elect a CPA to handle your tax prep and related deductions. An S Corp may also be subject to an additional tax depending on the state it operates in.

LLC

An LLC is an entity that many freelancers find themselves relying on, as it is the most suitable, most popular and most convenient. It is not nearly as costly as it is to form an S Corp, and it comes with a great deal of protection for your personal assets. And you'll also avoid paying both personal and business taxes on your income.

Income and expenses related to your LLC get reported on your personal tax return, as you're the owner and operator of the business. To go further, an LLC is much better where debt is involved than an S Corp and much more flexible.

In order to establish your business entity, you'll just need to file the appropriate form and pay a minimal charge to your state's Department of Financial Institutions – most of which can be done directly online or printed directly from the website. Do some research to find the best way to do file in your state!

CO TIP:

Your personal Chief Operator will help guide you through the process from beginning to end in forming your LLC. Visit www.and.co for more details.

Choose your business name

Setting up your business is tied greatly to how that business will appear to others. That is why choosing a business name goes hand and hand with determining your business entity. You want to think carefully about the name and then you need to protect it.

We advise you to pick a domain name early as most businesses should absolutely establish an online presence. Try to make your domain the same as that of your business. While you may not set up a website immediately, reserve the name by registering your site as soon as you can. Check availability of the domain you want to use through www.register.com.

If you operate the business under your name, as do many freelance writers and business consultants, you can skip this step. However, if you operate under a fictitious name, you should register it by declaring "doing business as" or DBA. Ultimately, you are required to register your business name, which prevents someone else from using the same name in your area. Check business name availability of your state online to make certain your name is obtainable.

It is also a good idea to gain legal protection for a business name so that no one else can use it. And this is particularly important if your business name becomes a brand. Get started trademarking your business, and frankly your brand, by visiting the U.S. Patent and Trademark website at www. uspto.gov.

Trademarking your business is just one step toward establishing the most vital parts of any business – a solid legal protection. Creating the documents that should accompany every project is another essential part of running your freelance business.

Draft a proposal

Begin each project with a proposal, which is quite simply a description of the work you'll be providing and the timeline in which you'll complete it. A quality proposal will help ensure that you and your client are on the same page right from the get-go. All proposals, no matter the length, should include these core elements:

- Overview of the project

- Timeline

- Deliverables

- Budget

- What's Considered to be out of scope (i.e. how many revisions will you complete?)

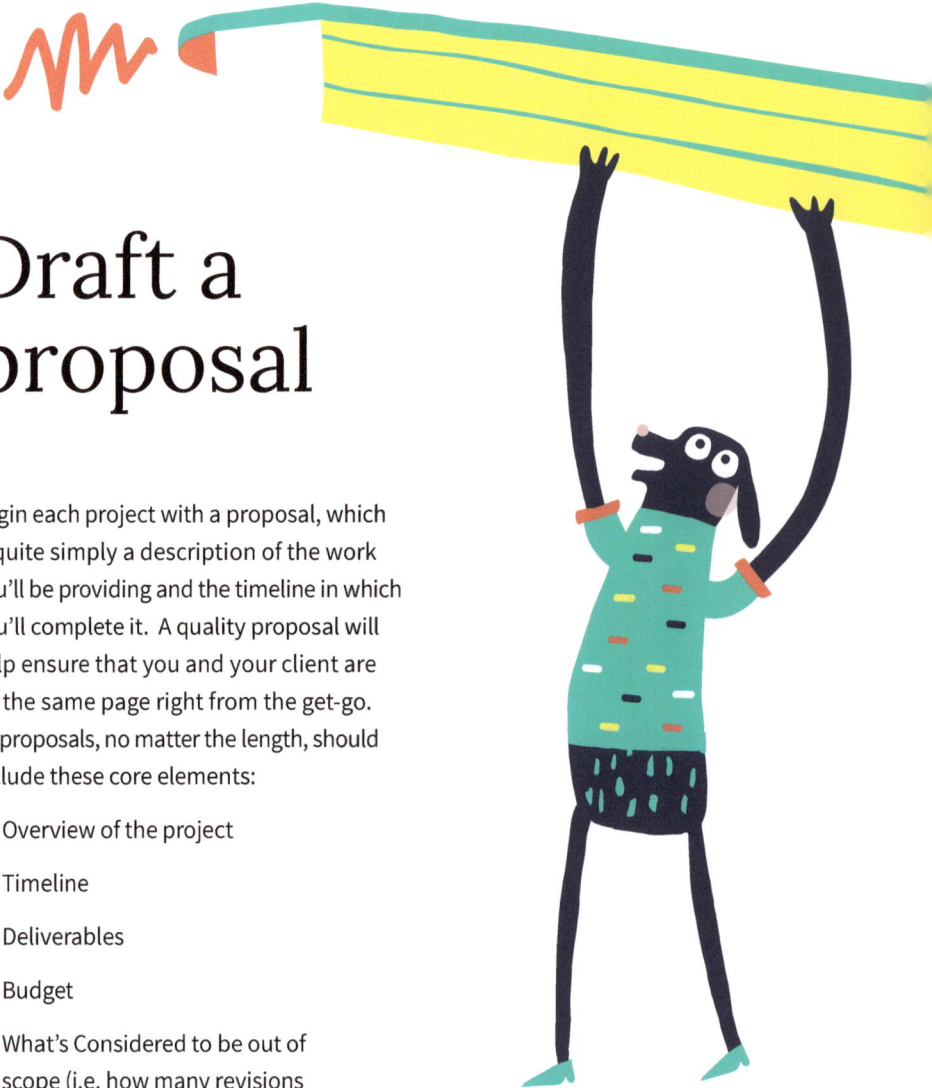

- Signatures

Craft a CSA and NDA

Along with a clearly stated proposal, you and your client should agree upon the details of your relationship in what is called Client Service Agreement (CSA).

This CSA generally includes the following:

- What your communication will look like, i.e. email? phone?

- How they can expect the work to be delivered

- Rights to intellectual property

- Payment expectations, i.e. how often? how much? what payment method?

Having both a proposal and CSA is truly best practice when it comes to running your freelance business with complete legal protection. And when your client is running their business with you in mind, they generally want for you to sign an Nondisclosure Agreement (NDA).

An NDA is a written agreement that guarantees you won't release any information that your client deems confidential. NDAs exist to protect both you and the client. As with any contract, if the NDA is provided to you by the client, make sure that you read the entire document carefully before signing on the dotted line – you need to know exactly what you're agreeing to.

Since you'll be utilizing these legal documents pretty frequently, it's advisable to have standard templates setup that you can tailor for each specific client. It'll make the entire process a little more manageable, and also save you some precious time.

Standard agreements are available for purchase throughout the internet and then you have the freedom to customize. We personally recommend asking your CO for a great one ;) You're also free to do some digging online in order to pull together your own versions in a simple Word document.

If you find yourself feeling stuck, enlist the help of a legal professional who specializes in this area. A payment is needed upfront, but you won't regret knowing you have all of your legal ducks in a row.

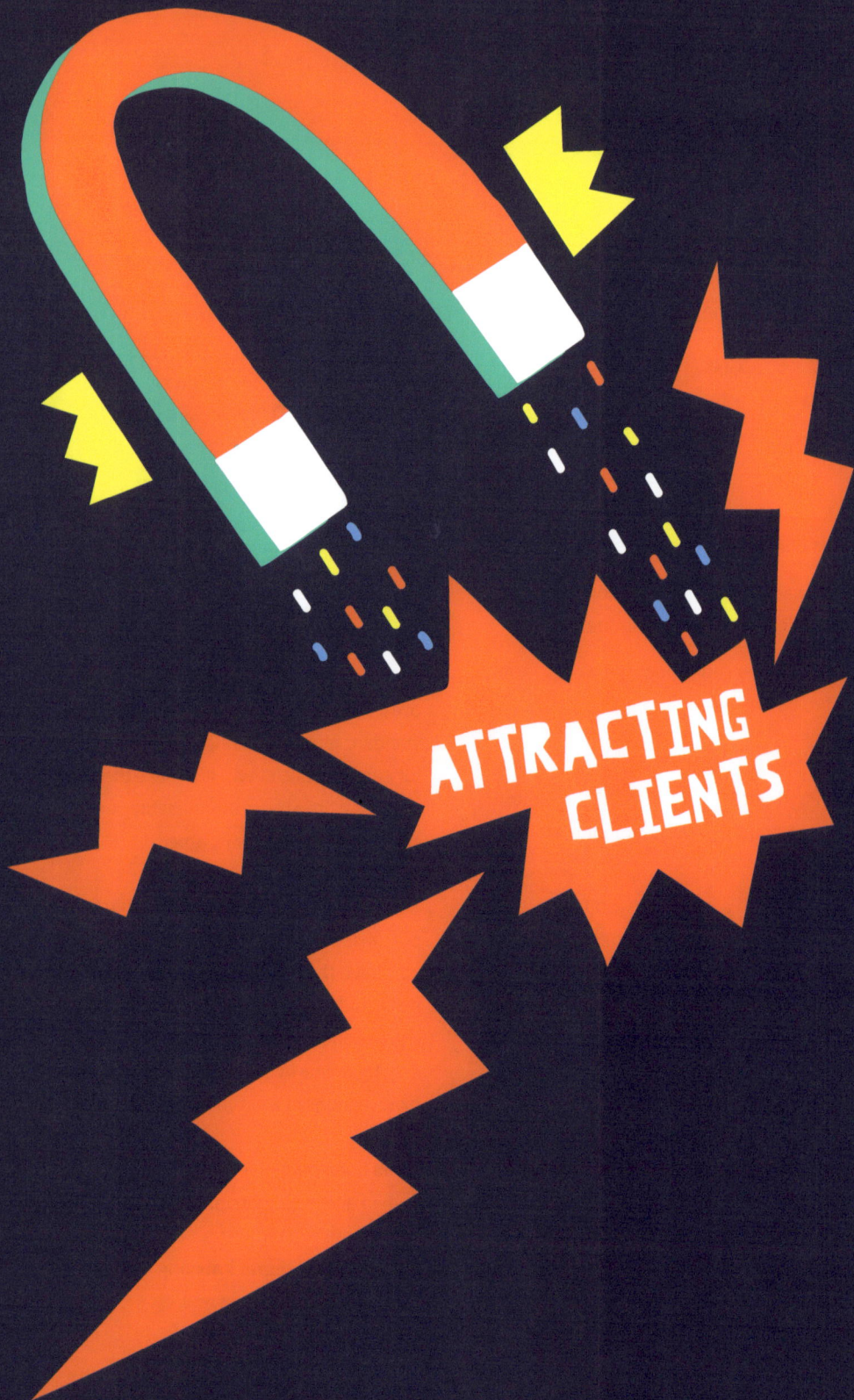
ATTRACTING CLIENTS

Identify your ideal client

Selling your services in a way that's effective and is uniquely you is an enormous part of the challenge to becoming an independent success. Here's the lowdown on how to make selling work for you. It all starts with some clients.

DO YOUR RESEARCH

Keep in mind: the goal is to get great work. Begin to build a list of businesses that answer the following questions:

1. Out of the clients I've most enjoyed working with, what was a common thread between them? Business size? Industry?

2. What is my passion? Is there a specific type of content I like to write, subject I like to photograph, or website I like to build?

3. Of the clients I've disliked, what traits did they have in common? What didn't I like about them?

CO TIP:

Create a public client wish list on your business website i.e. Nike, frog, Google, etc. This list will encourage target companies to reach out if they identify with one of those on your list.

IDENTIFY YOUR DEAL BREAKERS

It's important that you also take some time to consider your deal breakers. What will you absolutely not tolerate from a client, no matter how well-known their business or seemingly perfect their requests?

Perhaps budget is a big concern – meaning you're going to need to look at larger companies, rather than smaller startups. Maybe you need advanced warning of any work that need to get done with extremely short notice – that likely means you'll want to stay away from any news organizations or businesses that need to get to things in an incredibly timely manner.

Thinking of all of those things that will force you to say "thanks, but no thanks," isn't necessarily as fun as picturing the client of your dreams. It is, however, a necessary step to ensure you're focusing in on those clients that will be best for you and your freelance business in the long-run.

Finding strangers and discovering projects

Now you know what exactly you should be looking for when filtering through potential clients. But there's an even bigger question on the table: how do you find these clients? Surely, it can't be easy – otherwise everyone would be a wildly successful freelancer sitting on piles and piles of cash. Implementing the right systems and procedures will constantly generate and identify new opportunities. Check it out:

USE THE INTERNET AS YOUR SECRET WEAPON

When you think of sourcing leads for your freelance business, the internet will likely be one of the first places that pops into mind. First, use the information about your ideal client you identified earlier. Then apply that to your search to find companies. And here is a handy tool to find those clients you'll like to work with: www.myopportunity.com. Go ahead and send a friendly email introducing yourself, describing the services you offer, and emphasizing the value you provide. Cold emails will become a key part of your strategy as a freelancer.

SOURCE ASSOCIATIONS

Professional associations are another great way to not only meet like-minded freelancers in your industry, but also get linked up with different work opportunities. If you are looking for official associations, here is a brief list:

- Graphic Designers (aiga.org)
- Illustrators (theaoi.com)
- Copywriters and Editors (naiwe.com)
- Content Marketers (the-cma.com)
- IT Pros (aitp.org)

These groups are frequently looped in on different projects and work opportunities that you could be a great fit for. Plus, they often host events, workshops, and seminars that you could attend and put your new-found networking skills to the test.

If official associations are not your thing, find organizations such as Working not Working in New York City. These creative communities will empower you to network often, find colleagues, and inspire your work. Also an option is to get a desk in a coworking space like WeWork (www.wework.com) to get a support network. Check out the WeWork discount available to AND CO members.

ASK FOR REFERRALS

There's no form of marketing more powerful than word of mouth. Referrals will be key when it comes to generating leads and finding new clients. There are three different types of people who will likely refer you for freelance work (and, no, your mom doesn't count). These people include:

A PREVIOUS/CURRENT CLIENT
Happy clients are your best weapon as a freelancer. The world is small, and satisfied clients are the perfect people to provide testimonials for your service and refer you to their own connections.

ANOTHER FREELANCER
Yes, the freelancing world is competitive. But, there's also a lot of collaboration. This is why connecting with other freelancers can be so beneficial – they can refer you for projects they're too busy to take on themselves. And not only that! If your fellow freelancer has a complimentary skill set, such as a developer to your designer self, then you two can team up and take on the project together.

A NETWORKING CONTACT
While perhaps the least impactful referral of the three, having someone speak highly of you is still better than nothing. If one of your connections has an "in" somewhere and is willing to refer you, that can be helpful! Ask for referral by simply being forthright and letting your connections know that you'd appreciate them keeping you in mind if they hear of other opportunities that might be a good fit for you. And, of course, be willing to return the favor if and when the opportunity arises!

GET FEEDBACK

The most important part of freelancing is permanent growth. Unfortunately as a free-lancer you get very little feedback. Truthful reviews of your work can provide a way to identify both your weaknesses and your strengths – creating potential new paths for becoming more competitive in your field.

Build "project reviews" or "check-in" meetings into the project plan. This can be either in-person or virtual. The number and timing vary by type of work, but a first check-in meeting should generally be held after the project is well under way, early enough, however, to course-correct if there are issues. A good rule of thumb is to schedule the first check-in meeting for when the project will be 25-30% complete.

A second check-in meeting is usually held when the project is 50-75% complete. These meetings don't need to be long or formal. The goal is to figure out if the client thinks the project and deliverables are on track, if the process and methods used to manage the project and do the work are effective, and to find out if the client has any issues or concerns.

A formal feedback meeting should also be held once the project is complete. The goal of this meeting is to ensure that the project requirements have been met and to understand any problems the client has had with the process or deliverables. It's also an opportunity to discuss possible follow-on ideas that add value to your client and extend the relationship. Be sure to go into formal feedback sessions prepared.

Prior to the meeting, develop a list of questions you'd like to have answered. Don't formally interview your client, but work these questions into the conversation. A good feedback session is a lot like a jazz performance – a combination of scripted parts and improvisation. Think through what your client may ask, problems she may point to, or issues that may be brought up. "War game" the meeting ahead of time, so you can anticipate what the client might say and prepare your responses ahead of time.

After any formal feedback session, review the key points for valuable takeaways. Be sure to send an email to your client thanking him or her and summarizing any action items or project changes decided upon in meetings, to show that you listened and that you're taking action.

And don't forget to collect more informal feedback along the way. This can be done via a combination of listening and occasionally asking open-ended questions such as "How does this look?" or "How are we doing so far?" or "Do you have any concerns?" Open-ended questions give the client more room for interpretation, and generally lead to more information than closed-ended questions. One important caveat is not to ask for informal feedback too often, or you risk having your client see you as a pest. Every situation is different, so there are no hard and fast rules about frequency, but checking in informally several times during a project is certainly not too much.

CO TIP:

Use a paid invoice to send a thank you and also to ask for a referral! Helps big time :)

SENDING THAT FIRST COLD EMAIL

You've identified your ideal client. You've got names and emails of people you know you should speak with. There is only one last step to take in order to secure a new project:

send a cold email. And as you may know, a cold email is called such because you do not know the person you are emailing. But ultimately, you can change the email into a warm introduction to your business and services. Let's break down how to go about that process right here!

INTRODUCTION

Reach out and initiate a conversation with the business you're hoping to work for. Your introductory message needs to be short and sweet. Emphasize who you are, what you do, how you can help this person, and then include any relevant samples, a link to your portfolio, etc. And don't forget to add a dash of your personality!

PROPOSAL

If the prospective client liked what they saw in your introduction, they'll continue the conversation about potential projects you could work on. Now you must pull in some of those more logistical elements we discussed earlier – particularly your rate, how you prefer to work and communicate, and other details that the client would need to know to determine if you're a good fit to work together.

To put your most professional foot forward, it's best if you pull this all together in a polished proposal. A PDF branded with your name and logo is preferable. But, even including this information in the body of an email would suffice – just ensure that the information is organized and makes it easy for the prospective client to zone right in on the information they need.

CO TIP:

As a CO, I see many proposals each and every day. It would be wise to get a second pair of eyes to review it just to make sure you're getting all the legal protection that you deserve. And if you need help in crafting one, text your Chief Operator. Afterall, someone has to watch your back.

FOLLOW UP

Prospective clients are busy managing other aspects of their business or drowning in a sea of proposals from your competitors. So, don't expect to hear back immediately. This is where the art of the effective follow up comes into play. If you haven't heard anything back on your proposal in approximately 10 businesses days, touch base again!

Keep a running list of the prospects you intend to reach out to, have contacted, and have initiated proposals with, including key information like contact name, last date of correspondence, and what action is needed next.

You can track this information using a simple spreadsheet, Streak.com or even Trello.com (which allows you to assign deadlines). Bottom line: Ensure that no matter what system you have in place to stay on top of your prospects and know when you're due to touch base again.

The price is right

Pricing shouldn't be scary, it's just a part of business. Let's dive into two of the business models that exist. Begin by picking which general pricing structure suits your industry and skills at the present time.

MARKET PRICING

A quick glance at a site like Upwork will show you how varied prices range across different regions. If you dive into the economics of it, the cost for a nice meal in North America could often feed a family for a week in Southeast Asia or some parts of Europe. As such, the market rates in comparison to international freelancers can be quite alarming.

That said, recognizing that most clients are looking for services from people in their region, you need to understand the local or national market. It's here where you may lose a deal based solely on the pricing strategy you've taken. If two freelancers are both offering the same services and both are considered equal in terms of skill and experience, but one charges $100 an hour while the other charges $20, there's no way the one charging $100/hr will win the project.

If you've just left the comfort of a traditional office, this structure may make most sense to you. And if you're a solopreneur who spends the majority of your billable time hammering out the goods, it's a great option. Think graphic designers or transcriptionists, rather than consultants or marketers. In this case, you'll also have to research based on external factors, such as location and experience level, rather than just bare-bones cost of goods and target profit margins.

PERCEPTION PRICING

Value driven pricing is when you base a product or service's price on how much the target audience believes it is worth. For example, if your client is a company doing hundreds of millions per year in revenue and they want you to redesign their website, the right design, messaging and execution could result in a significant return on invest-ment. As such, you want to ensure that what they pay for the website is commensurate with the value you deliver. If you've become a force in your freelance niche, this pricing model is best for you. Within this model, you'll leverage your unique skills to com-mand a higher rate. Be prepared to have case studies or demonstrable experience to back your quotes. A hefty social media following doesn't hurt either, since you can also promote yourself as an influencer.

With either pricing model, you will have to consider five important things. Be sure to check off the following:

1. DEMAND
Pricing according to the demand and the economy. If there isn't much demand or if there is an economic slump, you'll want to make certain you aren't pricing too high.

2. OVERHEAD
Keeping your lights on is a critical component of pricing. Calculate your yearly utilities, wifi, heat, rent/mortgage, marketing and insurance costs. If your project is one month, divide everything by twelve and you'll know how much your overhead costs.

3. BILLABLE TIME
Knowing how long certain tasks take you is extremely important. You should always be able to estimate a baseline or reference point for your project pricing, whether you bill per hour or not (more on that in just a bit!).

4. BILLABLE EXPENSES
Regardless of your area of expertise, there will be supplies, equipment and necessary expenses related to your project work. Record those! And bill them appropriately to your clients. It's their domain name, ad space, or photo rights after all.

5. PROFIT
Consider your talent and expertise when it comes to pricing your services. But bottom line your profit is what you are charging over and above your expenses. Determine the yearly salary for your needs and then begin to calculate your desired profit goals (typically 10%-20% more than your salary).

CO TIP:

Whether you're a writer, consultant, or web designer, pick the business pricing option that makes the most sense for your work. Test the waters early on by trying both pricing structures discussed. Your business is going to evolve, so if your first option does not work out, give the other a try! But no matter which option you ultimately decide on, your pricing needs to sustain your busi-ness and allow you to earn each and every penny you're worth.

PICK YOUR RATE

Whether you choose to price your services via the market or perception, it makes sense to keep an eye on the clock while you work and know how much time you spend on your work (or writing emails, making phone calls, tweets etc.). And all the while time flies by, your business depends on the price tag attached to those seconds, minutes, and hours. You have a few choices, and it comes down to you in making the final decision. The question really comes down to two different roads to take. Let's explore the pros and cons of both.

HOURLY BASED RATE

To be frank, hourly pricing is simpler. And it is something you are already going to do while you are working on all your projects (elbow nudge). Hourly rates are also useful if you are doing a small, short term project. It could also benefit you if you are working with a client over a long term period or on an ongoing basis. When project goals and timelines are unclear, choose to charge hourly – that way your client will be forced to respect your time and consider clarifying the project. Get paid easier for items outside the original scope of the project by billing an hourly rate.

But clients may be wary of the rate if there is no project ceiling. Ask the client about budget expectations before you quote an hourly rate! If the project proves to be very demanding, your hourly rate typically needs to be adjusted and that may result in negotiations which will be very challenging – hourly rate adjustment is a much harder sell. If you are fast, then your hourly rates do not take this into account! It may be difficult to raise your hourly rate, especially if your clients are coming from referrals. Clients will mention your hourly rates to each other when they refer you! Lastly, if your client does not understand the work that you do they may see the activities listed on your invoice and be confounded why it took you so long to do something that seems simple.

PER PROJECT RATE

By charging per project, you can tailor your rate to the project and the client. Further, you can predict income much more easily by billing per project as you won't be estimating the amount of time it takes you to do something. You have the flexibility to include packages for different services you offer which allow you to vary the rate. Charging per project allows you to increase your rates easiest and test out your market's tolerance for higher rates.

A per project policy for rate intuitively shows your clients that there are multiple factors going into your pricing. Further, charging per project maximizes your income because you become limited only by how quickly you can finish the work. You'll find productivity incentives soaring and ways to do things quicker as a result of per project rates. And that allows for extra time to search for new clients, which means more work and more profit!

It can be a challenge to calculate a project rate though. And that could take time which is a precious resource. And the more time you take, the higher chance you'll have at losing the project to a quicker bid. Again, go back to the five necessities above: demand, overhead, billable time, billable expenses, and profit! If you are the type of person who is nervous to ask for more money, per project rates cause you to lose out on money in the long run especially if scope creep becomes an issue.

Overall, many freelancers use a combination of the hourly rate and per project rate. For example, you may choose to set a project rate for the work outlined in your scope and contract agreement, and then you charge an hourly rate for any work required outside the original set of terms.

Defining feedback loops in your project schedule is a must, that way you avoid project fuzziness throughout the entire working relationship. It is also recommended that you stick to the schedule agreed upon between you and your client.

Ultimately, make sure that your rate is high enough to allow you the flexibility needed in your new freelance life. And with regard to fully embracing your freelancing pursuits, make sure that you don't let any client treat you like a full timer aka long hours or rough tone. Communicate your point of view and your client will understand.

Remote work vs. on-site work

Remote work versus on-site work is a conflicting scenario, and both options have their advantages and disadvantages.

REMOTE	VS	ON-SITE

REMOTE	ON-SITE
Work on whatever project you like, whenever you like	Work only on that one client's project at the onsite location
Make your own schedule	Let the bossman make your schedule
Skype/Google Hangout etc. into meetings	Rub elbows with Bill from marketing at onsite meetings
Snag a beer at a local Meetup with a bunch of comrades or potential clients	Grab drinks at happy hour with the team after a long day of work onsite
Get a referral from one of the fellas you met at the Meetup the other night	Secure another follow up gig working with Bill in marketing onsite
All you need for work is your laptop, supplies, and internet	All you need for work is your car or public transit and a bright, shiny smile

Generally, working on-site does not allow you the chance to work on other projects at the same time. And when you prep a rate for onsite work, factor the costs of lost opportunity into the pricing. Keep in mind also that your schedule is out of your hands when you work onsite. Yet, you will most likely be able to expense your travel and meals.

On the other hand, working remotely lets you work on your own schedule, take on as many projects as you like, and dress in your pjs everyday.

Conversely, working onsite can strengthen relationships and build trust with a team that you would never have gotten the chance to truly interact with for 8 hours a day, 5 days a week. The better you know people personally, the more likely you will be hired again.

Starting off remote might hurt the possibility of re-hire, but maintaining constant communication and providing excellent work can easily allow you to jump that hurdle.

No matter what, you should always make your best effort to deliver outstanding work, create easy modes of communication with your client, build a relationship with your contacts, develop a workflow and feedback loop that suits you both, and ultimately let your passion shine through when working with your client so that those referrals will be a no brainer.

CO TIP:

Quote your client a rate that includes fewer zeroes. A specific number, such as $2,763.00, shows that you made the effort to actually calculate costs rather than a round number (i.e. $2,700.00) that looks padded. Price your services right, honestly, and deliver them in a proper proposal. Your client will see your respect for the work you do from the very start.

RUNNING YOUR
PROJECTS

A happy client makes a happy freelancer

At the core of being a freelancer is the work you do. Once you set aside all of those logistical elements of websites and branding and prospecting, your projects make up the meat and potatoes of what being a freelancer is all about.

A successful freelancer is not only talented – he or she is also organized, communicative, and able to deliver projects in a timely and thoughtful manner. As you already know, successfully managing your own projects is easier said than done. We've pulled together some helpful information you can use to complete projects in a streamlined way that's sure to keep your clients happy.

LEARN TO SCHEDULE

If you work on site, scheduling your work is a no brainer and feel free to skip straight to the briefing phase. If you don't happen to work on site, one of the most challenging elements of being a freelancer is attempting to figure out how much time each project is going to take you. When you're the only one responsible for managing and planning out your entire workload, you'll often find

yourself wishing for a crystal ball that could tell you just how much time to allocate to each and every piece of the puzzle.

While we can't fork over a handy crystal ball, we do have a different method that will help you be a little more realistic and organized with the way you approach your timelines: work-backs.

A work-back schedule starts from the date a project must be completed by, and then lists all of the related tasks in reverse chronological order – with a due date assigned to each of those tasks. By planning from the end to the beginning, you'll ensure that you outline a roadmap that not only breaks your project into separate milestones, but also helps you guarantee project delivery by the agreed-upon deadline. And that's a recipe sure to delight and satisfy your clients.

EACH CLIENT IS UNIQUE

No two clients are exactly the same. You'll find some that you click with perfectly, and others that prove to be a little more difficult. Regardless, it's up to you as the freelancer to make every effort to ensure the relationship is as seamless as possible. Here is the secret sauce to making client-relationship building the backbone of your business.

SET EXPECTATIONS EARLY

Many strained client relationships are simply the result of unclear expectations on either end. Emphasize the importance of your SOW and your CSA – which we discussed in an earlier chapter. Those documents will solidify in writing any areas for dispute with a client. Get on the same page from the start, and you're much more likely to set yourself up for success.

HAVE SYSTEMS IN PLACE

Having dedicated, formal systems in place can be such a help in making sure you work as efficiently as possible. You should attempt to systemize different parts of your business so that you can take care of these logistical elements with very little thought or effort. Here are some examples:

TEMPLATES
Set up template documents and canned emails that you can easily customize for each client. Save yourself hours by not starting from scratch each and every time. Here are some topics for the emails that you should have templated:

- Outreach
- Delivery
- Thank you
- Feedback
- Payment Received

ROUTINES
Pick set dates to conduct regular activities. For example, select Friday as the day each week when you'll send a friendly update email (using a saved email reply, of course!) to each of your clients and send your invoices out on the first of every month. Having a predictable schedule in place will save you tons of time.

ONBOARDING
Establish an onboarding system. Getting new clients up to speed and through all of the hoops of getting started with you can be a pain. Set up a system, using a tool like Trello.com, to ensure that your clients go through a set process.

TIME TRACKING
Be transparent and track your time. It is incredibly important to always keep your client in the loop and to make the communication as transparent as possible will lead to better, more satisfying work. Also, tracking time regardless of whether or not you are charging per time is a very good

idea. Keeping note of where your time is really going and having the evidence to present to your client what you have been working on is a powerful best practice you will never regret.

CO TIP:

While we advocate for templates to save precious time, you still want to ensure you're dedicating time to personalizing your correspondence. That personal touch is both necessary and appreciated!

WHEN IN DOUBT, OVER-COMMUNICATE.

While expectations for communication and progress updates will be outlined in your CSA, you need to hold yourself accountable. If you promised to communicate weekly, you stick to that schedule - your reputation and your business depends on how you handle the entire communication process. When in doubt, over-communicate. In the end, your client will be informed and will operate from a position of knowledge.

When a client reaches out on a weekend, reply asap. If it's urgent: act. Offer solutions, not excuses. And try to be cooperative. The client may reach out on a Saturday afternoon, that means you have a choice: reply that you will have a look first thing Monday morning or establish higher weekend rates. And don't forget to track time spent on work emails.

FINDING THE RIGHT TOOLS

From to-do list apps and project management systems to social media dashboards and integration tools, there's a seemingly endless amount of tools available to you – all of which promise to make your freelance life easier and more streamlined.

Getting your clients to use the same tools will make you more efficient. If you work on multiple projects, and one is in Asana and the other in Jira, that can be a pain. So aligning your tools with what your clients already use and/or get your clients to you what you chose can be awesome for efficiency.

We encourage you to be thoughtful and intentional about each and every new tool you bring into your workflow by asking yourself the following questions:

- What problem does this tool solve for me?

- Am I already using an existing tool that could solve that same problem?

- How will I utilize this tool on a daily or weekly basis?

BRIEFING AND RE-BRIEFING

It is important to define the scope – that initial briefing of the project and services you will be providing. Once established and agreed upon, it is crucial to re-visit the scope after work has been produced to make certain everything is still on target. Also, make sure to define feedback cycle and process. That may look like a Skype session scheduled weekly for Friday afternoons, or that may be a site visit for a catch-up meeting every other week. Whichever the method of feedback and the process for delivering it, stick to the schedule, honor your commitments, and deliver your best.

If and when the briefing or scope of the project changes, it's the client's choice. At that point, you will need to recalculate your fee and timeline. Add a cancellation fee and policy to your proposal initially and your butt will be covered. Ultimately, communication is key. Jump on a Google hangout often with your client. Become an essential part of their team. Make every effort to stay on the same page.

DELIVERING THE FINAL PRODUCT

All the tools in the world won't be able to supplement the actual delivery of your final project to the client. It is critical to discuss the final product because your client needs to feel that expectations were met and understands what you've completed. That way you are able to cement a positive relationship for future work (and those glowing referrals!).

Set up a time for both you and your client to briefly chat about your delivery. This one-on-one conversation will give you a chance to walk the client step-by-step through what you've completed, and also provide the opportunity to explain anything complex to them especially if you completed a complex project. Beyond that, this discussion will demonstrate that you're a conscientious freelancer who truly cares about the final product.

RECEIVING FEEDBACK

Depending on what is outlined in your proposal, you may need to respond to feedback and complete revisions for the client. Of course, you'd love if your clients told you, "Everything looks perfect!" each and every time you submitted something to them, but that isn't reality. Receiving constructive feedback isn't always easy, but responding to it effectively will be your secret weapon as a freelancer. Being open to suggestions for improvement and specific client requests will only make you better.

If a client isn't forthcoming with feedback, feel free to ask for it! With each piece of feedback, you will improve the quality of your projects, while simultaneously establishing you're someone who's always looking for chances to refine your craft and please your clients. And remember, never take business personal. It's hard. The work you do is you. You might have put everything into it. Still, it's business. Don't take it personal.

GET PAID FASTER

Getting paid late for hard work sucks. Make it as convenient as possible to get paid. Offering more payment options helps. Accept payments from credit cards, ACH or wire bank transfer, or PayPal.

Also have a rule for late payments. Before you start working, be very specific to mention a specific due date for each invoice and what fees will be applied once invoice is not paid on time. Be as clear as possible on what you have done for the project. Attach a timesheet if you charge tracked time, describe what you have done in detail, and even if you do not charge by time you'll have a complete overview of your work at the ready for your client.

CO TIP:

AND CO offers a PayMe Page to every member. On that PayMe Page you offer your preferred payment methods, including credit cards, ACH, and PayPal. Painless time tracking and beautiful invoices are also available to all AND CO members.

WHEN THINGS GO BAD

Unfortunately, there are some projects that just don't work out. Keep calm and stick to courtesy, class, and the utmost professionalism. The secrets to executing a graceful end of a professional relationship are knowing when it is time to call it quits, where to go from there, and what to send in that final email and invoice. Let's take a deep dive into how to answer those questions.

WHEN TO CALL IT QUITS

Circumstances that encourage you to walk away from a client relationship can vary greatly (and can run the gamut from understandable to totally terrible). Here are some clear indicators that you and a client should part ways:

- The rate is no longer competitive with your other work.

- The client has always been slow to pay (or still hasn't paid) for your work.

- You've shifted your focus, and the client no longer fits in with your new approach.

- Communicating with the client has been a constant battle.

Where to go from here? Again, this can vary from client to client (depending on the exact circumstance you're in). However, these general steps should provide a guide you can follow no matter the scenario:

STOP ALL WORK

First things first, when you know you're going to be putting the brakes on a client relationship, you should stop all work for the client. This step is especially important if your client is far behind on payment (there's no use racking up more billable hours that you might not be compensated for).

There is an exception to the rule here. If you're in the middle of a big project and are going to wait until after you've wrapped up those loose ends to go separate ways from your client, you should by all means finish up the project as promised.

HAVE THE CONVERSATION

Needing to tell a client you're hitting the road is enough to send a nauseous feeling from your stomach to your throat. Take a deep breath and remember that this is business – you aren't the first person to move on, and you won't be the last.

If you can have this conversation in person or over the phone, that's always preferable to sending a "Dear John" type of email. You're free to provide some reasoning if you choose to give the client some context, but don't feel the need to be overly detailed here. You don't need to make excuses for yourself.

SEND THE FINAL INVOICE

During the conversation just described, you should make it clear to your client that you'll be sending along a final invoice for any outstanding work that you need to be compensated for.

Pass that invoice along with a friendly email. And, be sure to include your payment terms one more time, just for good measure.

BE GRACIOUS

Above all else, it's important that you remember to be gracious and appreciative for the opportunity. This client was willing to work with you and pay for what you had to offer (when you were just getting started no less!), and that deserves your heartfelt appreciation. Beyond that, your reputation is one of your biggest assets in the freelance world. So, even if you're leaving that client behind, you want to make sure you leave them with only positive things to say about you.

Why marketing matters

Even if the work you deliver to clients doesn't involve a lick of marketing, maintaining your business will! Here are the most effective methods of marketing your freelance business and how to easily execute them.

Leverage testimonials

Your past clients will have a huge influence on your business and the health of your marketing. Word travels fast, no matter how large the community around you appears.

Strive to leverage testimonials from clients with whom you've had success. After having worked with a freelancer, the majority of clients are accustomed to delivering testimonials. Often clients will be honored to have an impact on the success of your company and be happy to contribute. It is best practice to lend a helping hand to clients who wish to provide a testimonial.

We recommend giving them the following questions to use as a guide:

- What was enjoyable about working with (your name)?

- What problem was (your name) working to solve?

- How has (your name)'s work impacted (client's) business

CO TIP:

Good ol' fashioned word of mouth should be a standby for your freelance business marketing strategy. Get those clients chatting about you.

The last time you got paid late, might have been the last time you got paid late.

Freelance smarter. From Proposal to Payment – AND CO is all you need.

JOIN FREE
www.and.co

AND CO

Get yourself out there

This topic alone could be an entire book, so we will just scratch the surface here to make sure you're not missing the obvious opportunities.

YOUR BRAND

You have to build your own brand. Why? Well, there's no more hiding behind a big, well-known company name, a professional corporate logo, and a formal brand that's been polished through years and years of hard work and refinement. Instead, it's just you. You are your entire brand. You just need to figure out how to spread the word.

When it comes to telling your story and getting your name out there as a freelancer, there are two main methods you'll want to make use of: Social Media and Content Marketing.

SOCIAL MEDIA

Social media is a huge part of the world we live in today. When you're trying to gather clients, build up a professional presence, and make a name for yourself as a freelancer. It's going to become an even bigger part of your daily life.

Now, nobody's saying that you need to buckle down and create a complex, multi-page social media strategy for your freelance business. There's no need to make things more complicated than they need to be. However, while you don't need to have a documented, formal blueprint in place, it's important that you at least have some sort of game plan to remain active and engaged in the space.

Try these simple social media tweaks:

- Brush up your LinkedIn profile by listing your new role as a freelancer, sharing some of your recent gigs, and even posting some of your most brag-worthy work.

- If you've written something lately, post it on LinkedIn. Share it with your network and become top of mind again.

- Craft a Twitter bio that shares who you are, what you do, and what exactly you love about it.

- Make it short and sweet. Use string of threes when describing yourself. And stay true to your business brand.

- Follow and connect with influencers in your industry.

- Set a goal to connect with at least 2 influencers every day or 10 a week. Like their posts, leave a comment, or retweet their content.

CONTENT MARKETING

"Content is king" - it's a phrase heard over and over again in the marketing world. And, while you might think it only applies to large and well-known businesses with established blogs, content can also be a powerful tool to help you grow your own brand as a freelancer.

I know what you're thinking: "But, I'm not going to be a freelance writer! Surely, this content rule can't apply to me as well."

Well, yes, content is especially helpful if you're aiming to make a name for yourself in the writing world. But designers, developers, photographers, and the like shouldn't count themselves out simply because they aren't making their living with the written word – content can be just as powerful for you.

Why? To put it simply, authoring content gets your name, your brand, and your expertise out in front of more eyeballs. Sharing information helps to establish you as a thought leader in the space. And, what client wouldn't want to hire someone who appears to be an expert in his or her industry?

So, now that you're convinced that content marketing is important, you're probably wondering how exactly to pull it off. Here are a few ideas to get the ball rolling:

GUEST BLOGGING

That industry-relevant blog that you've always followed and admired? Send an email to see if they accept posts from guest contributors. It'll offer great exposure.

YOUR OWN BLOG

If you aren't quite ready to reach out to someone else to publish your content, set up your own blog – either on its own or as part of your business website. You'll be able to blog about topics of your choosing, while also building a great platform you can share with potential clients.

PUBLISH ON MEDIUM

Or Pulse! If you haven't checked out these publishing platforms yet, you definitely should. They can be an effective way to generate both buzz and traffic.

Networking and relationship building

It's not always what you know, but who you know. It's advice you've heard time and time again – and for good reason. As a freelancer, your network is going to be one of your greatest assets when it comes to pulling in clients, landing new opportunities, and growing your business.

We've already talked about marketing yourself on social media. But, these outlets aren't only useful for self-promotion – they can also be an effective way to expand your web of professional contacts.

Done getting those social media profiles all polished up? Use your accounts to network – after all, your story doesn't do much good if there's nobody around to hear it.

Connect with business owners, industry peers, and even prospective clients on LinkedIn. Send complimentary tweets to people you want to spark a conversation with.

Social media presents a relatively low-pressure environment in which to build relationships – relationships that are sure to benefit you as you continue on this freelance journey. Want to step out from behind the screen and do things the old fashioned way? Of course, networking in person is still very much alive and well. In fact, tearing yourself away from your computer in order to get out and shake hands with some real people is encouraged.

This is how business is done. Activate or reactivate your network. Get in front of people, let them see you, and they'll hire you.

But, where do you find these chances to network? The opportunities are nearly endless, but here are some places you can start:

- Join your college's alumni association. There are always different events and seminars you could attend.

- Join industry-relevant LinkedIn groups (particularly some local to your area!) to be notified of related events.

- Join an area professional association. They frequently host networking events and mixers for their members.

- Check in with your local community college or other educational institution to stay informed of different workshops, seminars, and conferences.

Make it your goal to get out there as much as possible. You'll likely be surprised at how much and how quickly your network of connections grows.

How to ace a networking event

So now that you're convinced of the importance of getting out there and meeting new people, you're likely left with one big question: how do you knock those networking events out of the park? You don't want to be the person left bumbling through a half-hearted elevator pitch about your business or scribbling your email address on a soggy cocktail napkin.

You want to look polished, professional, and prepared. It's nothing complicated – it just takes a little bit of prior planning.

Here's what you need to know to make the most out of any networking opportunity.

BEFORE THE EVENT

As with anything, adequate preparation is key. Make sure you've crossed your t's and dotted your i's before strutting with confidence toward the appetizer table. Let's examine how to do exactly that:

GET BUSINESS CARDS

Start by making sure that you're armed and ready with some business cards. Remember, your goal with networking is to meet new people – so, you want them to have an easy way to get in touch with you even after you've waved goodbye.

Getting business cards for your freelance business is surprisingly easy, thanks to companies like www.vistaprint.com or www.moo.com. However, you'll want to ensure you leave enough time, so that you have them in hand by the time that event rolls around. What you put on your business card is totally up to you.

CO TIP:

AND CO members get access to a ton of great perks and discounts like a special deal at MOO.com! MOO allows customization of both sides of each card. Make sure the card fits in a wallet and has a spot for your client to write notes. Check: www.and.co/freelance-benefits

PREPARE YOUR ELEVATOR PITCH

A solid elevator pitch will include two simple components:

- What you do

- The value you provide

For example, if you're starting your business as a freelance content marketer, introduce yourself with something like, "Nice to meet you, I'm Jason. I'm a freelance content marketer who helps businesses build their brands and engage their audiences through thoughtful, valuable content."

Keep it simple and straightforward. Share your enthusiasm for the work you do and express interest in learning about the individual you are speaking with by asking, "what system do you currently have in place for engaging your audience?" If you are interested in what they are doing, then the more intrigued they will be in understanding how you can help them.

DURING THE EVENT

Strive to accomplish these two tasks during the event:

Strike Up Conversations

Don't wait for people to come up to you. Instead, grab the bull by the horns and start conversations yourself. Ask what s/he does for a living. Find out how s/he came to know about the networking event. Bring up an interesting article you read that afternoon. Do what you can to get the conversation rolling. After all, getting started is the hardest part.

Sell Potential Clients

Use that elevator pitch you prepared before the event to share what you do and the value it brings to the table in a way that's natural. Be sure to leave people with your business cards and encourage them to reach out if they find themselves searching for some help in your area. You might just be surprised at how many calls and emails you get after the event comes to a close.

AFTER THE EVENT

Networking is all about relationship building. Your work isn't over just because you've exited the event. Following the event, make certain to do the following to further strengthen the relationships you began to kindle:

Connect via Social Media

As mentioned earlier, your goal is to make a relationship. Head home and begin connecting online with the people you met at the event. LinkedIn is your best place to start. Since you walked away with a business card (if you heeded our advice), you have a full name and even a job title you can use to find that person on LinkedIn. Search his or her name and send a personalized connection request. Be sure to explain how much you enjoyed meeting him or her, and that you're looking forward to staying in touch. Now you have a low-pressure, convenient way to touch base if and when you need to.

Record Notes

Jot down some personalized notes on the back of each business card. Taking that extra step to scribble down a few notes will ensure you have helpful information that you can use to not only strengthen that relationship in the future, but also demonstrate that you were actively engaged in the conversation.

I like big bucks and I can not lie

We've got the nitty gritty on what you need to know right here.

Being able to earn a living and pay your bills with freelancing can be a thrill. In that regard, "money" is an amazing word associated with your freelance life. When you start thinking about accounting, taxes, expenses, retirement, and cash flow, suddenly "money" becomes one of the absolute scariest words you can associate with freelancing.

We get it – as much as you love cashing those hard-earned client checks, all of the other financial aspects of your business aren't quite as exciting. They could be quite dreadful (unless you're a freelance accountant or financial planner, that is).

Managing the financial side of your business can be enough to inspire you to hide under your desk (particularly if you don't consider yourself a numbers person). As you might guess, keeping tabs on cash flow is crucial for the health and well-being of your business.

Open separate bank accounts

Setting up the proper accounts right from the get-go can help to instantly simplify your finances.

To start, open a designated business checking account, which should include a debit or credit card for all purchases, specifically for your freelance business. Deposit any checks you've earned and make any business-related purchases with this account. Keeping everything in one account will make things much easier for you come tax time. Trust us on this one. Seriously. Do it today.

Aside from a checking account you can use just for your business, you'll also want to explore your options for retirement savings as a freelancer. It's in your best interest to open up a retirement account (such as an IRA) as soon as possible. Not only will this give you the vessel you need to begin planning for your own retirement, but it will also allow for you to move a portion of your income into your retirement account each year, which results in a pretty big tax break for you.

In addition to a business checking and IRA, open up a business savings account dedicated to setting money aside for tax time. Remember, taxes aren't subtracted from your income automatically anymore. You need to be ready to pay quarterly taxes, as well as your yearly tax obligation. Consciously save for those tax payments - trust us!

CO TIP:

Check out the AND CO quarterly tax calculator to get to the bottom of your payment obligation: www.quarterlytaxcalculator.com

Save while spending

One of the best parts of being a freelancer is the fact that you can write-off your business related expenses. This includes everything from office supplies to marketing expenses, professional fees, and continuing education. Basically, if it relates to your business, chances are you can include it as a tax write-off.

Here are a few popular categories of deductible expenses, for your reference:

- Office Supplies/Furniture, i.e. standing desk
- Mileage/Transportation, i.e. 40 mi round trip to client presentation
- Reference and Research Material, i.e. book on UX/UI design as a freelance designer
- Equipment and Software, i.e. GitHub as a freelance developer
- Professional Fees, AIGA as a freelance architect
- Phone and Internet, i.e. Verizon bill
- Postage, i.e. USPS stamps
- Insurance, i.e. Blue Cross Blue Shield health and dental insurance
- Travel, i.e. United Airline ticket to your new client's headquarters
- Marketing and Promotion, i.e. Facebook ads
- Legal/Tax Preparation Fees, i.e. CPA fees

That is by no means an exhaustive list, but it illustrates that there are numerous deductible expenses you can be taking advantage of. Keep track of those (with that business checking account!) – they'll provide a great help when tax time rolls around.

CO TIP:

Save money by filing all expenses correctly or rather have it done by your CO. For some freelancers like designers, even going to the movies or a Spotify subscription can be tax deductible which may save you up to 50% of costs. Ask your CO that comes with a free AND CO membership!

What exactly is a write-off?

When you pay taxes, you only pay them on your taxable income. Taxable income looks a little something like this:

Total Income	$60,000	$60,000
Expenses		$15,000
Taxable income	$60,000	$45,000
Taxes (35%)	$21,000	$15,750
Profit	$39,000	$44,250

+ $5,250

So, let's say you made $60,000 freelancing in one year. However, you had $15,000 in deductible expenses. Instead of needing to pay taxes on $60,000, you'd only need to pay on $45,000. That's $15,000 less, which means you'll owe significantly less!

Keeping adequate track of these expenses can bump you into a lower tax bracket as well, further decreasing the amount you need to pay. Seems worth keeping track of now, right?!

How you should track your expenses

If you're thinking this all sounds too good to be true, we assure you, it's not. However, it does involve organization and planning on your end.

As you might guess, you need a record of every single business-related purchase you make – and even categorize them. Heads up, shameless plug: AND CO does this automatically for you – it's as simple as it sounds. Connect your business bank account and watch magic happen.

If you're not a fan of magic or more time for freelance work, no hard feelings. You can also start a simple spreadsheet to track your expenses. Just make sure to keep note of the following things:

- Date of Purchase

- Amount of Purchase

- Purpose of Purchase

You also need proof of every single business purchase you've made over $75 in the form of a receipt. Hang on to every single one of those pesky slips of paper. Even if you pay for something in cash, ask if you can get a purchase receipt for your records. These receipts are especially important if you ever find yourself being audited. AND CO also solves this mess, as you are able to upload pictures of your receipts directly to the app.

But if you prefer to stick with old fashioned methods, your best bet is to purchase a large 12-pocket accordion file with a pocket for each month. Slip your receipts into the appropriate pocket as you accumulate them and have them relatively organized for tax time.

How often to invoice

When you're just getting started as a freelancer, you will need to determine the frequency in which you send your invoices. It is a personal decision, but with AND CO and the ability to work nearly anywhere, we recommend that as soon as you've rolled your sleeves down and finished your work – invoice!

Before you send an invoice, you and your client should both have a common understanding of your payment structure. This information should all be detailed in your CSA that was signed when you first began work. It never hurts to reiterate those expectations when submitting your very first invoice for payment.

If you'd prefer to send an invoice at the conclusion of a large project rather than waiting for a date to roll around, that's perfectly acceptable. In this case, ensure that you and your client are on the same page about when they should expect to receive that invoice from you. Clearly and constantly communicating will pave a path to success.

CO TIP:

The frequency of invoicing is ultimately up to you and your client, but you should always choose a standard before engaging with your client. That way you can speak from a position of knowledge and confidence. A Chief Operator will handle creating an invoice at every appropriate time; resend outstanding invoices; and mark invoices paid as soon as funds have been received.

Accepting payments

It's also important that you determine what forms of payments you'll accept from your clients. Clear payments options are the key to a simple, timely client transaction. And as a reminder, the AND CO PayMe Page allows for three key payment methods, which means that you're likely to get paid much faster i.e. the more options of payment you provide, the more likely your client can satisfy one of those.

COMMON PAYMENT METHODS

Let's take a look at a quick rundown of the pros and cons of each type of payment:

	PROS	CONS
PAYPAL	• Convenient and free for your clients • Very secure • Easy to transfer money directly to your bank account	• Fees: PayPal charges 2.9% plus $0.30 for each transaction and 3.9% + a currency conversion fee for international transactions
CREDIT CARD	• Convenient for your clients • May be used with PayPal	• Many laws and security precautions that you need to keep track of • Processing fees: Stripe charges 2.9% + 30¢ per transaction.
CHECK	• No associated fees • Relatively easy for you to deposit into your own bank account • Paper trail	• Can be inconvenient to expect your clients to mail you a check • Waiting period to receive payment in the mail

CO TIP:

Get paid faster: AND CO offers every member their own PayMe Page. On this page, clients can pay via the preferred payment methods whether that be credit card, ACH, or PayPal.

What if a client doesn't pay?

Get started by organizing all of the documentation you'll need to prove that you're entitled to that money you're owed – that includes gathering correspondence between you and your main point of contact, those contracts and documents you had signed in the beginning (here's your SOW and CSA coming into play again), as well as any invoices that are still unpaid.

GO HIGHER UP

Take that information and approach someone higher up within the company. Perhaps it's just your contact that's flakey and unreliable – and not the business as a whole. Talk with someone higher up the food chain and see if you can get the issue resolved that way.

SPREAD THE WORD

If the previous options fail, share your experience. Hopefully you will help other freelancers avoid falling into the same trap.

"Wait, shouldn't I lawyer up and go after what I deserve?" you're likely thinking to yourself now. It's advice you've likely heard time and time again. Unless you're owed a large sum of money (over $10,000 is typically a good benchmark), the cost of legal fees, travel, and lost work time likely won't be worth it in the end.

KEEPING GOOD COMPANY WITH THE IRS

Why you have to pay taxes?

Quite simply, everybody does it. Think about it: If you were employed full-time or even part-time, those tax payments would be taken directly from your paycheck. But, as a self-employed freelancer, you're responsible for making those payments for income tax and self-employment tax yourself. Luckily, you don't have to pay it all at once. Instead, you satisfy this responsibility by making quarterly tax payments.

When to pay taxes

When most people think of taxes, they likely think of April 15th. But, if you're a freelancer, you'll likely need to be making tax payments every quarter. Those dates are roughly those listed below but can differ from year to year:

- January 15th
- September 15th
- June 15th
- April 15th

Paying quarterly is the best way to handle your freelance business tax burden. But if you happen to miss a payment, you have the option of making a larger payment come the next quarter or paying more in yearly taxes. If you choose not to pay at any of the quarterly deadlines, you will have to write one hefty check at year's end and you will also be subject to penalties for skipping quarterly payments.

CO TIP:

Chief Operators remind freelancers about approaching quarterly tax deadlines, deliver income statements before every quarter, and assist with quarterly payment calculation via www.quarterlytaxcalculator.com

How much you have to earn to pay taxes

There's a common misconception in the freelancing world. And, that is, that if any one client pays you less than $600, you don't need to report that income and pay taxes on it. However, spoiler alert: That's simply not true.

According to the IRS, all income earned through a business is self-employment income, which is definitely fully taxable and must be reported. So, don't get tricked into thinking you can slide those smaller payments under the rug – it's not a good idea.

To put it simply: Any money you earn through your freelance business needs to be taxed. There's no way around that.

However, self-employment tax may be avoided if your net profit is below $400 for the year. But, if you're freelancing for a living, you'll likely never meet that requirement.

How to pay your taxes

Paying your taxes really isn't as complicated as many people make it out to be. In fact, you simply need to fill in your information on a straightforward payment voucher, write your check, and mail it to the instructed address.

To pay your federal quarterly taxes, you can grab Form 1040-ES directly from the IRS website, print the payment vouchers you need, and get it taken care of.

To pay your state taxes, you'll need to find the appropriate form through your state's Department of Revenue. Search online for your state's name and "quarterly tax form", and you should get right what you need.

Remember to keep a record of how much you paid, as well – you'll need that at the end of the year.

CO TIP:

Every AND CO member receives an income statement - a detailed statement of income from projects and freelance work including a complete description of expenses listed in the appropriate tax deductible category.

Designer,
Entrepreneur,
Accountant.
Yeah, right... ;)

Freelance smarter. From Proposal to
Payment – AND CO is all you need.

BEING PRODUCTIVE

Time is money

Never is that statement more true than when you're working as a freelancer. When your income is so directly tied to the hours you spend working, you undoubtedly want to make the most of your time and, thus, maximize your income. You can work faster – but only so much; you can charge more – but only so much. Service doesn't scale. Be aware and make the most out of your time.

Learn to prioritize

Automate what you can

You've heard people go on and on about the importance of prioritization. And for good reason. It's an essential skill if you're aiming to best leverage your time.

As a freelancer, you're solely responsible for your entire workload. You'll need to learn to differentiate between the urgent and the important. When in doubt, your best bet is to prioritize based on deadline.

Prioritizing just based on deadline ensures that you're always tackling your to-dos in a systematic, strategic order. And even better, it'll help you never miss a deadline!

As we talked about earlier, your actual projects don't always account for the largest chunk of your workday. Instead, it's those pesky, repetitive tasks that manage to add together and eat up all of your hours. But, if those tasks are so simple, why do you need to be the one spending time doing them? Explore solutions like IFTTT or Zapier to automate tasks you find yourself completing on a routine basis – such as automatically saving email attachments to Google Drive. Use Boomerang to send emails at times that you are away from your desk and to remind yourself to follow up with clients or potential business.

Also explore hiring a virtual assistant to manage many of your administrative tasks. Or – cough, cough – here at AND CO, we like to think we do a pretty good job of lessening the freelancer's workload.

Establish business hours

Construct a working schedule that fits you best. If you are most productive during the afternoon and evening hours, make it clear to your clients that you will be available to correspond during this time and this time only. You determine your working hours. Just be sure to communicate that to your clients.

One way to ensure that clients respect your time is respond to emails, texts, slack messages (or whichever preferred method of communication) during your business hours. When you stick to your schedule, your clients will learn and follow accordingly. And if you happen to find a client who does not choose to respect your schedule, then you should politely reiterate your hours of availability.

Avoid distractions

Working from home is nice. But, it also comes with it's fair share of distractions. You could start that load of laundry or empty the dishwasher instead of answering some emails. You could walk the dog instead of beginning that project. Or, you could binge on Netflix instead of sitting in front of your computer.

Distractions are ever-present. So, it's going to be up to you to do your best to avoid them. Keep in mind that super quiet places may not inspire you, but that all depends on the tasks at hand. Diamonds are created under pressure so try to have at least two projects running at a time, because frankly this may improve your output!

Not every freelancer works from home or a coffee shop or a hipster cafe in Brooklyn. Some freelancers work on site, in an office, or in co-working spaces. You have to find a place where you are most productive and where you could truly focus on your work. Finding those spots that work best are best discovered through trial and error. Ultimately, decide on a space where you're free to do your best work. And wherever that may be, you will have to fight distraction of some sort. Try a solution like StayFocusd to keep you away from the black hole of YouTube or Facebook. Or take a stab at the Pomodoro Technique. This time management method breaks your work day into intervals – 25 minutes spent working, followed by a five minute break. Each of these time chunks is called a "pomodoro". By splitting up your workday, you're prompting a sense of urgency. Rather than thinking you have hours and hours to complete that assignment, you'll try to get as much done as possible in your 25 minutes. Plus, it's a great reminder to stand up and step away from your desk every now and then. Embrace your natural tendencies and habits. Being yourself and finding your flow will allow for your best work to come to life.

Remember why you chose freelancing

It is no doubt that you are starting your freelance business in order to gain more freedom – this book is called Welcome To Your Independence, no less. So we imagine that you value the time you spend with family, friends, and loved ones.

As you embark on this freelancing journey and leap triumphantly toward your goals, prepare those individuals closest to you that you will need their support and help (and don't forget to add you truly appreciate it).

Remember to demonstrate to your family and loved ones that they matter and that you care. Proactively schedule calendar time with them. Keep your phone on silent when you are together. These are great practices even when you aren't a super busy freelancer.

When it comes to sustaining your freelancing life, make sure to consistently evolve. Staying competitive and updating your skillset will not only keep you constantly interested in your business, but it will also make you a true contender for the most desirable projects. Pick classes that challenge you.

Attend conference meetings that enlighten and empower your business. Distribute funds toward that stuff (it is less expensive than you think #taxdeductible).

Get a helicopter view frequently and evaluate your direction. It is easy to get dragged down by day to day craziness. Here are the things freelancers can do and should do to stay inspired:

- Take frequent holiday / off-season where prices are cheaper

- Do work from remote places

- Work other hours than 9am-5pm to grow and learn

- Take time and resources to fund sideprojects and passions

- Reach out into new fields

- Learn new things, even unrelated to your business

- Dedicate time for your children

- Spend time with your family

- Look at business politics and useless meetings with a smile

- Take the freedom to say no to projects that are not beneficial to you

- Seize these opportunities that full timers do not have

- Have fun!!!

It is very likely that making a living is not the only reason why you wish to go freelance. At the beginning of this book, we asked you to think long and hard about why you want to go freelance. And then we asked for you to write those reasons on a piece of paper. Stay true to that big picture. Each year, refine the reasons. And never lose sight of what makes you who you are or the passion you have for the work you do.

**SHARE YOUR LOVE.
WORK HARD.
FREELANCE SMART.**

Welcome To Your Independence

The Freelance Handbook

Editors

Amanda Spinelli

Martin Strutz

Writers

Amanda Spinelli

Kaysie Garza

Kat Kuehl Boogaard

Illustrations & Layout

Basia Grzybowska

Martin Strutz

Disclaimer: This book is a collection of professional advice from experienced humans. However, the information in this book does not imply any legalities or responsibility on the part of the writers, editors or AND CO.

Copyright © 2016 AND CO Ventures Inc. All Rights Reserved.

www.and.co

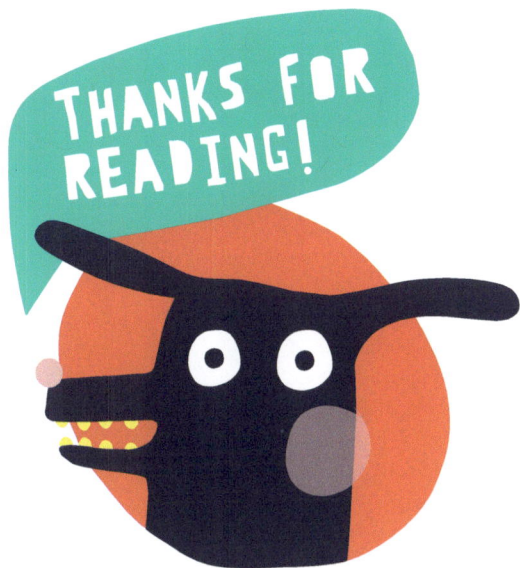

www.ingramcontent.com/pod-product-compliance
Lightning Source LLC
Chambersburg PA
CBHW041146210326
41519CB00046B/155